Sniper Marketing

Kishore Dharmarajan

DEDICATION

To my kids who think I am messing around with a laptop at all times and my
wife who thinks I am on to something important.

ACKNOWLEDGMENTS

To every marketer who has gone before me, especially the digitally savvy ones

CONTENTS

KISHORE DHARMARAJAN

WHO ARE THE WORLD'S GREATEST MARKETERS?

Have you heard of a guy called Frank Kern? If you haven't you should check him out online. This dude made a cool 25 million dollars in a few days time selling a course called 'Mass Control' that teaches people how to control minds and take over markets.

Then, there is this chap called Jeff Walker, who came up with a brilliant concept called 'Product Launch Formula' which triggered off a 100 million dollar affiliate industry.

Every time Apple launches a new product, they use a systematic marketing approach that is very similar to what is being taught by Jeff.

The third chap I want to introduce is Tim Ferriss, the author of the 'Four Hour Work Week' and 'The Four Hour Body'. Have you noticed that his first book has got nothing to do with is second one and that his writings are based on market demand?

Tim is a smart writer, who has figured out that you discover markets first and then cater to it. Unlike most writers who spend a lifetime writing about what they love and sell 25 copies with great difficulty.

So, what do these smart new marketers have that conventional marketers lack? How are they able to take a blog post and turn into a viral message that gets reported in the Huffington Post?

How do they write a simple email that gets read by thousands of people across the world?

How do they create successful products and services with no marketing budgets? And more importantly how do they create a piece of content that generates millions of dollars in revenue in the space of a few hours?

Sniper Marketing is going to expose some of the best kept marketing secrets of the decade and introduce concepts that you never knew existed.

If you are a marketing manager, you can use these concepts to unleash a highly cost-effective, yet powerful marketing campaign for your product or service.

And if you happen to be a small business owner or online marketer, the lessons that you learn here will be invaluable in generating leads, extra business and extra profit. The whole book may feel like a joyride of information. So sit tight and enjoy the Ride.

WHAT IS THEIR SECRET WEAPON?

G oogle gets over 2 billion searches a day. These searches are done by real people sitting on their laptops or smart phones searching for information from around the world.

If you think about it, you can see that no person would take the effort to go to Google and search for a particular piece of information if they weren't REALLY looking for it.

Unlike the normal browsing we do, were we may spend a lot of time reading gossip or chatting with friends, Search is a need-driven activity and leaves clues into our psyche.

A search term is an itch or a condensed need that we enter into the search engine and we expect the search engine to provide all the answers.

I like to think of Google as an 'Hospital' where we go when we are sick and need answers, while I see 'Facebook' as a shopping mall where we hang out with friends. This is precisely why B2B ads work on Google while B2C ads far better on Facebook.

Every search term that is entered into Google is indexed in their enormous datacenters, not as an individual term but as part of a profile of the searcher. Which means the Search Engine is trying to understand the searcher as a whole and not in isolation.

All the large search engines like Google, Yahoo and MSN collect and compile online data to better understand their user and their needs, but also share these details with their advertisers who can use this online intelligence to serve relevant ads.

If I have been searching for Tennis news on Google, I will start seeing tennis related or at least sports related ads when I move through Google's content network (which is blogs and sites with adsense ads). If I get an email on Gmail that talks about NBA, I can expect to see a basketball related ad on the side.

This is the great online intelligence at work, which I call The Great Online Brain. There is so much information out there that the smart marketer has only to go online and tap this enormous resource of data to build extremely focused marketing messages.

Let's say you have a headache and you went online to do some research about headaches. You might explore a bit and find out that what you have is not a normal headache but a migraine. Now you go online and start searching for information on migrates.

You understand the causes of migraines and you also understand that there is treatment available for it, but more importantly you learn about a medication called 'Imitrax', which seems to be efficient in treating migraines.

The third time you go into the search engine, you are typing in 'where to buy Imitrax' and you are much more informed than when you were searching in the first or second instance.

You went from searching for 'headaches' to 'do I have a migraine' and ended up with the search term 'where to buy Imitrax'.

In Sniper Marketing terms, you progressed from a Prospective Customer with a Need, to a Prospective Customer with Information and ended up as a Purchase Ready Prospect or PRP.

This is one of the key principles that underground Marketing Giants really understand and use. While mass marketers buy traditional media space in TV and national print and go after large populations, the really smart marketers differentiate between prospects with needs and prospects with dire needs.

The next step is to differentiate between prospects with dire-needs and purchase-ready-prospects.

At any given time, only a tiny portion of an entire target group will be purchase-ready-prospects and sniper marketing is all about identifying that golden segment. The massive advantage of sniper marketing is that once you identify the PRP, you can almost ignore the rest and save immense amounts of marketing time, energy and spend.

*
*
*

I like to think of Google as an 'Hospital' where we go when we are sick and need answers, while I see 'Facebook' as a shopping mall where we hang out with friends.

*
*
*

SNIPER MARKETING

HOW SMART MARKETERS WIN

I magine you are the marketing director of a firm and you have been assigned a specific budget to attract a fixed number of prospects for your company's new line of fashion-ware.

In the pre-internet era, you would have looked at demographics, done media sampling and sent out a test direct mailer to gauge the market. Once you have the metrics, you would have rolled out a larger campaign using the daily press, radio, outdoor and if budget permitted the TV.

Years later, with the rise of the digital media, you'd still be doing the same stuff. Most marketers and advertising agencies assume that digital is another media to reach the consumer. They take their offline (TV, Print, and Radio) creatives and turn them into banner ads and videos for digital distribution. This is the stupidest thing that can be done.

Digital is not a new media, it is a new world when people are expressing their deepest concerns, their fears, their passion, their innermost thoughts, their opinions, their anger, their love – everything that makes human beings tick.

Smart marketers like Frank, Jeff and Tim have come to use the power of the Great Online Brain and read people's mind. And when they do that it is very easy for them to talk, convince and sell.

With this powerful info at their fingertips, it is very easy for them to transition from a mass marketer to being a warm friend who understands the problems faced by their target. When they assume the position of a trusted advisor or expert, very little selling is required even when high priced products are being sold.

I am sure; you can see where we are going with all of these concepts. Smart Marketers don't go after the mass market as a whole. They tend to concentrate on a small portion (20%) of their target audience, which they know will yield (80%) of their sales.

If you are not familiar with the 80/20 principle, I recommend you have a look at the book 'The 80/20 Principle by Richard Koch. You will quickly realize that everything we do in life is connected to the 80/20 principle and marketing is no different.

The 80/20 principle states that 80% of all results come from 20% of efforts, and if you can find out which 20% of your efforts are working, it makes sense to concentrate on that portion and ignore the 80% unproductive efforts.

What makes the 80/20 principle so powerful is that using the digital space you can structure a marketing program or an entire business around a simple calculation that 80% of your sales will come from 20% of your prospects.

Which means 5% of your buyers will drive half your profits and that you will sell at least one product or service every time you get 2000 targeted visitors to your site.

Isn't it amazing thing that you can predict your sales (and if you are the imaginary marketing that we discussed before, you can get back to your management and show them your expected sales based on your marketing budget?)

If I confused you with the math, let us recap once again. 80% of your profits come from 20% of your customers and if you apply the 80/20 calculation to the top 20% you will see that 5% of buyer will drive half your profits. The online world has a 1% conversion rate, which means one in every 2000 prospects turn out to be a buyer.

The Sniper Marketing strategy that is being used by the world's most effective marketers is all about going after that crucial 1% of your prospects. There are three advantages when you do that.

Firstly, you saved the massive amount of marketing spend that you would have wasted in going after the worthless 99% of your prospects.

Secondly, since you used the Great Online Brain to read the minds of the 1%, you know exactly what they want and your marketing process can be finely tuned to closing the sale.

Thirdly, of the 1% of customers that you gained, there is another 80/20 sub group that can be taken advantage off. That is, 20% of the customers who bought your stuff can be upsold to the next level, while the remaining 80% may respond to down-selling. In both scenarios, you upped your profits by another 200% with no extra effort.

If all this theory sounds complex, you are not alone. Most people take some time to get around these concepts. But once these ideas sink in and you see the examples that I have, you will be shocked the marketing world never knew these strategies existed.

You might have also noticed that the PRP that we were talking about in Chapter 2 and the 20% that we discussed in chapter 3 are the one and the same. It is no coincidence, but pure marketing genius that the marketers who discovered these principles have been exploiting its power to the hilt.

(By the way, there is another aspect to the 80/20 rule that sniper marketing doesn't touch on. This is the effectiveness part of the 80/20 rule which we don't go into in Sniper Marketing. If you are interested, it goes on something like this:

The 80/20 principle is more than just a handy rule of the thumb; it is a powerful principle that works on top of itself to produce a cascading effect of successive gains.

Let's say you've got 10 product lines. The 80/20 rule says, the top two will generate 80% of your business and the other eight only generate 20%. What that really means is that the top two are SIXTEEN TIMES more effective than the other eight. The effective group brings in four times as much sale with one fourth of the resources.

So the 80/20 rule isn't about 10% improvements, it is potentially about 1600% improvements and more. It isn't about fine-tuning things, it is about making potentially very small but fundamental shifts in the structure of your business and getting huge returns on your effort.

And it is not just 16X improvements. Because there is still a top 20% of the top 20% (4%) that produces 80% of the 80% (64%). So 4% of your effort produces 64% of your results.

Then there is another top 20%. 0.8% of your effort produces 52% of your results.

And another top 20%. 0.2% of your effort produces 40% of your results. That means if you double the effectiveness of the most important 1% of your business. That is if you change a tiny part of your marketing, advertising, customer services or operations – your results go up not by 2% or 10%. IT GOES UP BY 50%.)

*
*
*

5% of your buyers will drive half your profits.

*
*
*

SNIPER MARKETING

IDENTIFYING PURCHASE-READY-PROSPECTS

U nlike most marketing systems that rely on theory, the Sniper

Marketing System is an exact science with step-by-step procedures which can be followed.

Let us assume, we have been assigned the task to market a new headache remedy to the world and following the principles of Sniper Marketing, we go on a journey to discover our PRP are and how we can target them with 100% accuracy.

Our first step in this journey starts with mighty Google itself.

We head to Google's external keyword tool (which is a free online tool) and put in our keyword 'headache'. Within seconds Google spews out hundreds of keywords that are being used by millions of Google users from around the world.

When we download this keyword data and sort it in excel, we begin to see the fantastic outline of a new marketing story. We see that people around the world have been searching for stuff like: 'migraine headache causes', 'migraine headache cures', 'Types of Headaches', 'Tension Headache', 'Headache Cure', 'Headache Treatment'.

What is Google trying to tell us here? Remember, they get 2 Billion searches a day and pretty much everything we are looking for is being tracked by Google.

Which means, if we figure out how Google is indexing all the billions of sites out there and co-relating that information with the billions of searches that happen on a daily basis, we can figure out to a large extent what mankind is thinking about?

Notice that I put in the keyword 'Headache' and seconds later Google suggests that keyword is too broad for commercial purposes and that I would have a better success, if used a keyword like 'Migraine headache cures.'

In one stroke we have discovered that prospective customers start out with keywords like 'Headache' but after doing some searches online they realize what they have is a migraine and then their search evolves into something like 'Migraine headache causes'.

So, to conclude prospective customers search for 'headaches', while PRP searches for long-term keywords like 'Migraine headache cures.'

Now, let's head to Google Insights:

Insights tell us that that keyword 'Headache' gets a lot of searches in the US, followed by Nepal, Canada and South Africa. If we are doing a global launch for our imaginary headache remedy, we know which countries would be ideal for targeting.

The next part of the research comes from Twitter. We land on a site called www.tweetgrid.com (you can also use tweetdeck.com) and put in the long tail keywords that we gathered from Google.

The moment, we put in keywords like 'migraine headache cure', 'depression headache', 'whiplash headache', we start to see a ton of live results from people who are on twitter and talking about that topic.

If you spend a few minutes on tweetgrid, you can get an idea about what people are talking about these keywords.

This is stuff coming from the other side of the wall and pretty powerful. Actual users are sharing their experience with you and if you are a smart marketer you will have no problem picking up the points of difference that can put you ahead of the rest of the crowd.

The insights from TweeGrid, combined with the interest groups gained from Google form the basis of the Sniper Marketing Strategy. If you are on a budget and want to get quick results.

The next step would be to setup a Google Adwords Search Campaign for each of the interest group that you have unearthed.

There are two types of ads on Google Adwords – Search advertising which happens on the search engine and Display advertising which consists of banners ads on blogs and websites.

Sniper Marketing works only with Search Advertising as you are trying to find out what is going on through the PRP's mind with your keyword based ads.

A quick campaign with six different search ads talking the language of the PRP and answering their needs, would in a few hours time give you the exact roadmap to create a highly profitable marketing campaign.

Remember, your landing page and the content on your landing page has to exactly match the tone and intent of the adwords ad. Which means, if your ad had asked the question (Struggling with Whiplash Headaches?), your landing page will be something like (I too suffered with Whiplash Headaches, but here is how I Got Rid of It)

Create separate ads and separate landing pages for each interest group and look at the impressions, clicks, optins and clickthrough rates. A quick look at the percentages will reveal the depth and breadth of your market.

It is amazing how little marketers use the power of online media to uncover consumer insights, but once you start to do it and begin to use Sniper Marketing Strategies you can see your market as if you are wearing one of those X-Ray Goggles.

*
*
*

Sniper Marketing works only with Search Advertising.

*
*
*

KISHORE DHARMARAJAN

DOES SNIPER MARKETING WORK IN REAL LIFE?

My friend Chris sells insecticide. The chemicals are bottled in a nearby factory and sold in local supermarkets. Since all the raw materials are sourced locally, his costs are low and he competes with the larger players with his lower cost.

Margins are thin in the chemical industry and when the recession came, he was kind of stuck between the large players who had dropped their prices and his own fixed costs.

Many of you who have your own small business might have faced this same situation, where you are caught between your competition and your own fixed cost. Even larger players face the same quandary at some point of their marketing evolution.

In the case of Chris, he had two options: Drop down prices further to take a temporary loss hoping to ride the recession or stop production all together and windup now.

When I met Chris, I gave him a third option. I told him, "If you can't reduce your prices further, then raise it up." Chris thought I had gone crazy, but since he had no option, he gave it a try and here is what happened:

Step 1:

We went around to the shops that were selling his insecticide and spent some time speaking with shoppers who were looking for insecticide. We got some great insights just speaking to these people.

Step 2:

We went online and searched for 'insecticide' on Google. We discovered that prospects were not looking for any insecticide. They were looking for specific solutions:

Customers were looking for organic garden insecticides
Customers were looking for organic insecticides for tomatoes
Customers wanted to kill cockroaches

Step 3:

We went to tweetgrid and Google Insights to take our research to the next level. We had discovered that there were four interest groups out there and we wanted to know what the Purchase-Ready-Prospect were looking for.

Obviously, they had progressed from prospects to prospects with information and had evolved into PRP.

With the insights gathered from the online tools, we had a good idea of what was going on in the heads of 20% of the market (PRP) who would bring us 80% of our sales.

Step 4:

We created a document that contained all the information that we had gathered from our online research and proceeded to create his new marketing blueprint.

The most important development that came out of the blueprint, was that instead of a single brand of insecticide, we created four brands that were aimed squarely at four different PRPs.

Brand 1: Organic Insecticides that won't harm pets
Brand 2: Organic Garden Insecticides that won't affect plants

Brand 3: Organic Homemade Insecticides to protect Tomatoes
Brand 4: Extra Strong Cockroach Killing Insecticide

Step 5:

We designed new labels for his insecticides, and created specific leaflets. The leaflets went on to talk about the harm being caused to dogs, cats, hamsters and other house pets by the usage of strong pesticides and why the user needed an organic insecticide to safely get rid of insects.

We created four kinds of leaflets, each talking about one kind of product and the type of problem it solved.

We also created a Google Adwords campaign targeting the four different niches that targeted Chris's small town. (This is a topic on its own and this eBook doesn't have the scope to discuss Google Adwords.

In short, Adwords is the fastest way to get traffic to your site and the quickest way to test that traffic to see what customers want and your PRP desires. Extremely powerful stuff.)

And then we went on to distribute the leaflets in strategic locations. The generic leaflets went to the supermarkets, while the one for pets went to the homes of pet owners (list collected from local pet shop) and the leaflets for garden insecticides and tomato insecticides went to the home of garden owners (list picked from the local garden suppliers shop).

32

Oh yes, I forgot to mention, the prices of all the stuff was raised by 25%, because we were competing in niches that the big players hadn't ventured into with the kind of insights that we had.

Step 6:

We participated in local pet shows and gardening events with demonstration of our products. We showed the harm caused by powerful chemicals and contrasted that with the safe application of our own products.

All the insights that we had uncovered from our research was now put on display and we were speaking the language of the buyer. We reflected back to the PRP, what they had been voicing over the net and they loved it.

Even with the miniscule budget that we had, we on to double sales in the first six months of our Sniper Marketing and profits followed. It goes without saying that Chris was delighted beyond words.

*
*
*

Adwords is the fastest way to get traffic to your site and the quickest way to test that traffic to see what customers want.

*
*
*

SNIPER MARKETING

DOES SNIPER TAKING SNIPER MARKETING TO THE NEXT LEVEL

T here are two ways to amplify your message and move from your PRP to the next circle of friends and peep group that surround the PRP. Although Sniper Marketing is all about targeting your PRP, we also need to amplify our message to reach out to the 20% in the next layer of your target, so we can maximize our sales and our profits.

To amplify your message, you have two options:

Paid Options include PPC, PPV and Media Buys.
Organic Options includes SEO and Social Media.

36

Paid Option: PPC

Although the terms may sound confusing and complex, once we go through the system you will realize they are quite easy to grasp. PPC or pay per click is a system whereby you pay for every click that you get.

The largest and most effective PPC system out there is Google Adwords, but Yahoo and Bing also offer robust platforms for advertising on Google AdWords helps you connect with potential customers looking for products and services like yours.

You'll pick keywords related to your products and services, and choose how much you'd like to spend on each click on your ad.

Your text-based ads will appear in search results and on Google's content network based on your bids for keywords.

The AdWords keyword tool can help you pick the right words and phrases for your business, and AdWords does not set a minimum spending requirement, so you can start slow and adjust your budget as your business grows.

Pay per click advertising has made other forms of online advertising, such as CPM (Cost Per 1000 impressions), banners and classified ads, pale in comparison.

While they still have their place it is possible to spend money on these types of adverts and not see a single response in exchange.

Pay per click advertising is different. Your ad could be seen thousands of times by plenty of different people, but unless someone actually clicks on your advert you won't pay a cent for the privilege. In truth, AdWords advertising is heralding a whole new age of cost-effective online advertising.

With AdWords PPC advertising you only pay if someone clicks on your ad. With normal offline advertising you have to pay for people to see your ad whether or not they respond.

Paid Option: PPV

Pay per view marketing is buying pop-up or pop-under traffic from advertising networks that sell this type of ad inventory, but this is not just any ordinary pop-up traffic.

This form of traffic is extremely targeted because you have control over which targets you want to bid on to have your ad displayed. A target is simply a keyword, key phrase or domain URL that you choose to bid on.

You can buy PPV traffic for as little as $0.002 per impression, which makes this form of traffic incredibly cheap and cost effective.
The following is a list of the major PPV networks that you can buy traffic from.

http://www.adonnetwork.com

http://www.mediatraffic.com

http://www.trafficvance.com

http://www.leadimpact.com

http://www.directcpv.com

Paid Option: Media Buying

Online media buying is one of the most effective methods for driving highly qualified traffic directly to your website. This form of advertising serves to secure the most Internet real estate, while reaching out to potential guests at nearly every level of the consumer purchase cycle.

Executed correctly, online advertising can be your most efficient means of increasing website traffic, conversion rates, and ultimately, improving your overall ROI.

With a small budget and a little know-how, any hotelier or travel professional can plan and execute their own strategic linking campaign. The following online advertising guidelines are designed to help you capture market share and stay ahead in today's competitive online travel market.

When it comes to online marketing, preparation and research are two of the most important elements to ensure a campaign is successful.

The first few things to identify in the planning process are your need times, or instances where you may require additional marketing support and available budget.

Your unique need times may focus on such goals as guaranteeing 100% occupancy and higher ADRs during peak season, improving business during the off-season, or increasing overall brand awareness throughout the year.

Determining how much of your budget to allot towards online media purchasing will help you decide where to start looking for media partners.

As a general rule, your budget for online media buying should be a significant portion of your pay-per-click marketing budget, which in turn should be at least a quarter of your total marketing budget.

Another important item needed to formulate your online media plan is a list of your marketing objectives. The most critical question to answer is whether you will you seek overall brand awareness or a direct response from the audience.

We all want direct results, but it is usually a fine balance of brand recognition and direct selling that achieves long term results.

It is crucial to have a firm understanding of your strengths and weaknesses in order to pinpoint your individual marketing proposition, or unique selling point (USP).

The USP is a single feature or benefit that sets you apart from your competitors in the industry. It could be a distinct sense of luxury, a central location, resort and spa offerings, a famed golf course, wedding expertise, discounted rates, or a kid-friendly atmosphere, among others.

Here some of the best sources of Meda Buying that is available online:

1. Xtend Media – banner/display media buys

2. ValueClick – banners, display/media buys

3. Tatto Media – banners/display/media buys

4. AdFunky – Display/rich media, some high traffic inventory

5. Advertising.com – display/banners, media buys

6. Z5x.net – display banners, media buys, large inventory

7. Bnmla – banners, huge volume, good for female demo

8. ReduxMedia – Display, media buys, some good blog inventory

9. Rubicon Project – media buys, nice interface/inventory

10. AOL Advertising – variety of solutions on AOL inventory

11. PremiumAccess.com – premium banner ad network

12. AdJuggler – display/media buys

13. Right media (Yahoo) – self serve banner exchange

14. Technorati Media – banners

15. Federated Media – cpm banners on good inventory of sites

16. Collective.com – media buys, banners/display

17. Vibrant Media – inline contextual/rich ads, media buys

18. Microsoft Ad Network – microsoft banner display/media buys

19. Glam Media – media buys, display, very good inventory for female demo

20. CPXinteractive – banners/display, media buys

21. CBS Interactive – media buys on very high traffic CBS site inventory

22. Burst Media – banners/display/media buys

23. Dsnrmg.com – display, media buys, unknown quantity/quality

24. BannerConnect – media buys/banners, good european reach

25. Undertone.com – premium banners/display/media buys

26. Tribal Fusion – media buy banner network

27. EngageBDR – media buys on high traffic inventory

28. Specific Media – banners/video display, media buys

29. FOX Networks – banners on FOX properties

30. MediaWhiz – banners/display, media buys

31. Interclick – banners, high volume media buys

32. AdKnowledge – cheap ads, slow approvals

33. Tremor Media – media buys, good range of new formats

34. Traffic Marketplace – display/email ads, media buys

35. Adconian – video/banner ads, media buys2

Organic Option: Search Engine Optimization (SEO)

Search engines are an indispensable part of the Internet. According to online statistics1, Google logs 2 billion searches a day, which implies that many people rely on search engines for information.

Websites that are displayed on the first page of search results-and thus have high search rankings-receive significantly more visits than those that rank low for the same sets of keywords.

More visits, in turn, may translate into a higher number of customers for the former. Organic search traffic therefore contributes significantly to online marketing success and business growth.

Companies have strong incentives to improve their rankings, thus giving rise to the term SEO, search engine optimization. There are two types of search results-organic and paid search.

Organic results are gathered by search engines' web crawlers and ranked according to relevance to the search terms. A website that contains fresh, authoritative, and keyword-relevant content may rank high for specific keywords at no cost.

In contrast, paid results are listings that require a fee for the search engine to display their links for particular keywords. Paid search can become an ongoing expense, and a company loses traffic as soon as it stops paying.

Organic search not only is free but also helps a company accumulate its online visibility. Since search engines record ranking history, a company can always improve its website ranking by building on previous content.

Also, most people click on organic search results instead of paid advertisements, giving a business even more incentives to focus on organic search.

How to rank high on search engines, however, is rather complicated and constantly changing. Many factors contribute to the quality of a company website as perceived by a search engine.

Different search engines such as Google and Bing may rank the same website differently because they prioritize those factors differently, not mentioning they update their algorithms constantly.

Most factors that contribute to high search rankings, however, can be controlled and grouped into three categories: keywords, on-page SEO, and off-page SEO. Keyword Selection Keywords are words that a company website wants to be associated with on search engines.

A website that optimizes for certain keywords appears in search results when these keywords are searched. They are important because they convey a business searchers' intent, interest, or need.

To attract potential customers instead of random visitors, a company needs to understand what keywords potential buyers use to find the kinds of products or services it provides. Keyword selection is therefore key to a company's search ranking.

To identify keywords customers use to find its products or services, a business needs to brainstorm customer needs. A company can use three methods to understand customers' perception of its products or services: web analytics, customer survey, and competitors' content.

It can review current web analytics to see what keywords that bring searchers to the website are used most frequently. Customer interviews are another effective way of containing this information.

A business can ask what features, functions, or advantages customers associate with its products. Researching competitors' website content also helps a company understand what keywords their competitors are trying to rank for, which may in turn lead the company to brainstorm what keywords can differentiate it from competitors or are worth competing for.

After compiling a keyword glossary from research, a company can narrow its selection based on four criteria: category, popularity, competition, and relevance. For category, a company can divide its keyword collection into verbs, nouns, adjectives, and adverbs.

Since people tend to remember a company by no more than a few words in total, a company should focus on one to two keywords from each category per page. On the other hand, keywords from different categories may be used together to form a unique brand.

Popularity, competition, and relevance also help determine which keywords to use. Popularity refers to how many businesses want to be associated with a keyword. The more businesses rank for a keyword, the more popular and thus competitive it becomes.

Using popular keywords might not necessarily help improve a businesses' ranking since it needs to compete with many other websites for them. On the other hand, a company should avoid using words that are not competitive at all since non-competitive words tend to be rarely searched.

It is therefore important to find words that both uniquely describe a company's services and are commonly used. Specific, long-tail phrases are an effective solution. Long-tail keywords are more specific and target less competitive niche markets instead of highly competitive broad keywords.

Longtail phrases containing commonly used words may significantly improve a website's search ranking. On-Page SEO On-page search engine optimization is another major contributor to higher search rankings.

On-page SEO is the act of optimizing specific keywords on the most noticeable places of a website and making it search-engine friendly. An optimized website makes it easy for search engines to find and revisit it, crawl links, and read keyword phrases. Four elements, in turn, contribute to on-page SEO.

The first element is a site's "crawlability." The term refers to how easily a search engine can extract new content from a website. To make the website crawlable, a company should use text links-hyperlinks that contain texts- in navigation. Ajax, Javascript, and Flash are difficult to crawl, which means that search engines will display no results for a webpage containing content only in these formats.

Yet eliminating content in these formats simply because of their low crawlability is unnecessary. Multi-media content can provide useful information that is searchable as long as a company uses relevant text elsewhere on the site. URLs also determine the crawlability of a site.

A straightforward, concise URL containing keywords makes it easy for search engines to decipher what that page is about.

In contrast, a URL filled with question marks, numbers, and phrases irrelevant to the page content is less capable of providing useful information and thus less favored by search engines when people search for content related to that page.

It is also important to have a consistent URL to accrue SEO credit for a specific domain-search engines may not recognize that two slightly different URLs lead to the same webpage.

The second element is search visibility, which refers to whether search engines recognize the existence of a website. Changes in website design, content management system, or just one character in URL can destroy search visibility.

When undertaking content migration or URL update, a company can take several precautions to avoid a drop in search visibility. It can map old URLs onto new ones, identify top inbound link sources and ask them to change links if necessary, and build new inbound links to the new URLs.

A business can also employ permanent 301 redirects. A 301 redirect is the most efficient and search engine friendly method for webpage redirection. It enables a website to preserve its search engine ranking and thus visibility.

A business should also monitor site analytics including 404 not found errors and possible fluctuations in search engine rankings. With careful management and design, a site can both maintain and increase search visibility. Keyword optimization is the third contributing factor to on-page SEO.

Once a company decides which keywords to use, it needs to use them in the right places to help search engines identify them as keywords.

According to a survey of over 50 CEOs who have extensive knowledge of online marketing, keywords placed in the following locations have strong positive correlations with search rankings:

Page Title: Defines the title of a page. Keywords preferably should be used up front. o Name of a Root Domain (e.g. keyword.com)

Anchor Text in Links (e.g. www.abc.com/keyword 1+keyword 2)

Meta Description: often appears in Google search results to describe a link

Alt Text: text that describes an image Of course, keywords also need to appear in the body content on a company's website to reflect that these keywords authentically summarize information on a company website.

A side incentive for optimizing keywords is that they not only help with ranking but also may increase the click-through rate on search engines.

The more keywords in a link description match with search queries, the more relevant that link appears to searchers and the higher the click-through rate.

Businesses should be wary of using all keywords on one page, however, using all keywords in the meta keyword tag (a place that allows a business to provide additional text for crawler-based search engines) reveals to competitors what keywords a company is trying to rank for and might lead them to compete for the same words.

It is generally a good practice to focus on one keyword phrase or two per page and ensure that each page has a unique title tag, which reinforces the use of different keywords on different pages.

Off-Page SEO Off-page SEO, or link-building, is another decisive factor in search engine optimization. In fact, link-building constitutes 75% of what helps a site rank high in search engines.

Linkbuilding does not refer to creating links on a business's own website, however. Inbound links are the crucial contributor to improvement of a website's search ranking.

Inbound links refer to links embedded in the content of a website that link to another website which, in this case, refers to a company's website.

A high-quality inbound link is one embedded in an authoritative and relevant website. For instance, a link from a page on New York Times that discusses video production is considered high-quality to a video production blog.

The higher the quantity or quality of inbound links a page receives, the more credibility search engines assign to that page and the higher its ranking.

To acquire more inbound links, a business needs to first understand why others are willing to contribute links to its website.

A website is worth mentioning and linking to only when it provides resources or valuable content. Content creation is therefore important to link-building.

What constitutes good content for link-building is no different from that in general. Of course, the likelihood of acquiring inbound links increases with content promotion and optimization besides creation. Inbound links from third-party sources are not the only type of links that boost search ranking.

After all, it takes time to build a reputation of good content supply to draw inbound links.

A short-run solution for a business is to provide "inbound" links to itself: cross-linking internally. Content promotion on social media utilizes links to direct interested readers to the website, and embedding links to other relevant pages on a company website may also add "link love."

Businesses should prioritize inbound links over self-linking because the latter is not as valuable. When they do utilize self-linking, it is also important to appear authentic. It is appropriate to include links to pages where viewers of a certain page may find more value.

Otherwise, the appearance of self-promotion may dispel visitors from the website, leave them a bad impression, and cause them to never revisit.

Organic Option: Social Media - Facebook

With its millions of users worldwide, Facebook has undoubtedly become the leading social networking site and has become one of the best ways for marketers to reach their target market, regardless of age, gender or location.

There are 3 ways on how you can do marketing in Facebook: the use of pages, targeted advertising, and group creation.

Facebook pages work the same way as with the individual's profiles. They are often used by businesses, organizations, and public figures. Unlike a person's profile, a page doesn't have restrictions on the number of friends or fans. It's easy to set up but can be challenging to build a good fan base.

When setting a Facebook page, consider spicing up your information tab. This is equivalent to your official site's 'About Us' page. Keep it as casual as possible while including some of your company's most important information.

You can also provide customized content by using Facebook's version of the HTML, the FBML. You may use this FBML for creating land pages that would lead them to your special discounts/offers and perks of becoming a fan.

Aside from the FBML, you can draw more users to your page by running interesting contests and asking your current fans product/service-related questions.

Open-ended questions such as asking for an opinion on your new product idea can engage the users into an interesting discussion and can be a great way to inspire loyalty.

Setting up a page allows you to update your fans, be it with your new products or services. However, this must be done in moderation. Avoid posting irrelevant and spammy posts in your fans' walls for these are the surest ways of driving them away.

Other method of reaching your target market is by taking advantage of Facebook's targeted advertising program.

In this feature, you can target users base on the information they have on their profiles which may include location, gender, relationship status, age, birthday, likes, and interests. The ads can be run on a per-impression or per-click basis.

This targeted advertising program allows you to evaluate your advertising scheme as users/fans can rate your ads. Great ads can be responded with 'Likes' while those that don't appeal well to the fans may be removed.

Through this you can reassess and cite factors that will help you create more effective advertising schemes in the future. You can custom tailor your ads to suit your company's marketing needs.

Another great way to gain loyal followers is to create a group. Instead of creating a group specifically for your company, create one for the industry or niche where your company belongs.

The success of any online group lies on the participation of the members. Urge your fans to participate by holding an active discussion. But before you start posting, be sure that you state clearly the group's content policies and make sure that participants have seen and understood them.

One good thing about Facebook groups is that you can send bulk messages to all members. You may use this to send highlighted discussions in the group.

If you think you don't have the time to manage the group, you may instead join one that includes your target market. Joining groups has its own pros and cons.

The good thing about it is that it's a great strategy for building awareness but it has stricter policies. Reading/knowing the group's policies beforehand is deemed necessary to keep yourself in the group.

Most often facebook groups don't tolerate posts that include any commercial content. Violating this rule may lead you to be banned from the group.

The world is changing and so should be your marketing strategies. If you haven't tried Facebook marketing yet, then you certainly are missing a great opportunity to boost your traffic and consequently, your sales.

Organic Option: Social Media - Linkedin

LinkedIn is more than just a networking site for professionals. With the proper use of its features, anyone can use it to generate more revenue, create an abundance of quality leads, convert leads into happy customers, and even to find potential investors for your products or services.

By incorporating appropriate keywords in your LinkedIn profile, you can improve its ranking. The five main places where you can place your keyword include the Headline, Current Work Experience, Past Work Experience, Summary, and Specialties.

Improving your LinkedIn ranking makes your profile more visible not just among those in your niche but from other groups as well.

Your LinkedIn status can also be used to achieve your networking goals. Updating your status allows your 'connections' to be informed of your latest activities and/or events, which increases your chance of expanding your network of connections.

You can make the most of your status by means of using it to promote networking events, seminars, relevant and informative articles, and sites. Since LinkedIn only allows 140 characters, long URL can be shortened by submitting it to www.TinyUrl.com.

LinkedIn allows you to add contacts from your address book and even invite those who haven't signed up yet in LinkedIn. If you think these people can help you, then without hesitation, include them in your contact list. By expanding your network, you can make your profile look good and attract more opportunities.

At LinkedIn, you are given a chance to throw questions, give answers, and partake in different groups' discussion. These things are done in these 2 places: the Q&A section and the group discussion board.

Participating on these places has the following advantages: one is getting free information from experts and even from new connections, and second, you get to expand your overall network.

Also, by constantly providing helpful answers to group members, you establish a good reputation among your connections. You are perceived to be an expert in one field and that's a great way to attract more people from the group.

Groups are another part of LinkedIn that you shouldn't miss. Find groups that are relevant in your industry. By having more people in your network, the more likely you're going to succeed.

If you think you are capable enough to handle a group, then do it by all means. By creating a group in your niche, you are providing a constant flow of traffic.

As a founder, you are also perceived as a "thought leader" or "expert", increasing your chances of receiving invitations from the experts of the same niche.

LinkedIn has advanced applications by which you can make use of to keep your profile more appealing to the public. These include applications for Amazon, Blogging, Slide Share, Google Docs, and Polls.

Organic Option: Buzz Marketing

Studding your site with relevant content isn't enough to stand out from the crowd and get the traffic that you needed. In this modern time where the Internet is deemed to be the new TV, it's equally important to come out with content that's exciting, entertaining, and eye-catching.

Let's start with the headline. Creating your headline is one of the most challenging parts of content creation. Make it boring and you'll end up driving away your potential clients and blowing away your chance of getting a loyal group of followers.

Typical internet users and/or readers are impatient. When your headline doesn't catch their attention for a few seconds or so, then forget it.

They would never read the rest of your post, no matter how much effort you place in it. This is why, you have to make your headline as interesting as possible.

Examples of attention-grabbing headlines include 'The Secret of [blank] and 'Who Else Wants [blank]?' These headlines have become popular because they usually appeal to the very nature of human beings: the love for secrets and for fast solutions.

Aside from the headline, you should also invest on the content itself. Be direct and keep the content as interesting, simple, and short as possible. Avoid using small font size and include relevant images as possible especially on the content's intro.

If you want your content to go viral, then try coming up with power lists and make them appealing to as many people as possible. Use simple words and sentences without losing the entertainment value.

You can entice more readers in your blog or site by shifting your focus and by coming up with something unique, weird or different.

Individuals are naturally self-focused so by directing the focus of your article on your reader, the more likely that they're going to read it.

And if ever you run out of crazy ideas (just to make your post/content truly unique), simply think of James Moran – what would he probably do in your situation?

Remember KISS – keep it simple stupid.

SNIPER MARKETING

*
*
*

Paid Media is the Quickest Way to Gauge the Market in the Shortest Time Period.

*
*
*

SNIPER MARKETING

WHAT TO DO NEXT?

If you liked the Sniper Marketing System and want to put it in action for your product or service, but don't have the time and information to carry it out, you can always contact me for further information.

I do have a personal one-to-one consultancy service (although I must warn you it is not cheap), and we can sit down to see how your business can be improved and how we can double your profits.

I can be reached on 0097150 6986164 or by email on kishoreed@gmail.com or seogurukishore@gmail.com

SNIPER MARKETING

HOW TO END THE ONLINE - OFFLINE BATTLE?

I magine you are driving down the street and see a billboard that shows a man emptying his pocket. And the caption is: Being Ripped off by Banks? Visit www.bank.com for details.

You pass the same billboard twice everyday and keep seeing the same billboard, again and gain. Then you take a look at the newssheet at the local grocer and see the same guy emptying his pocket and the same caption staring at you. You tap into your smart phone and log into www.bank.com.

There is a nice story on this site about a man who got ripped off by several banks, till he found one particular bank which offered credit cards on very low interest rates.

Since you were recently taken for a ride by several banks, this story seems quite interesting to you and you fill-up the form on the site. In a couple of days, you get a call from the bank and they help you to sign-up for the bank's new credit card.

I hope you noticed what happened here. The mass media triggered off interest using interesting visuals on billboards and print ads.
The digital media picked up where the offline media stopped and went on to use the larger conversation space to build a story and case.

You cannot walk into a hall where a digital event is happening without hearing from the digital guys about the budget wastage created by using offline media.

You hear all about response rate, clickthroughs, conversions, lead capture, follow-up and return over investment.

While it is true that offline media cannot match the effectiveness and returns of online media, it has massive presence and volume that cannot be matched.

The Sniper Marketing Method uses the massive reach of offline media to trigger off interest (this is for larger companies, if you are a small business operating on a miniscule budget, I recommend you forget the offline part and go straight to the online marketing part).

Once offline media triggers off interest and takes the PRP to the website, you can use the larger conversation space of your web presence to build your story.

Remember, we are not talking about any story, we are going to build our case based on the points of difference that we gained by listening to customer-speak on tweetgrid and Google.

I hope you are beginning to see the power and logic of this incredible system that sucks the dreams and fears of customers and uses that very same information to create a powerful sales process.

Along the way, we eliminated customers and concentrated on the PRP, we also reduced our marketing budget and we even got rid of the constant battle between offline and online media.

The rest, I hope is marketing history.

ABOUT THE AUTHOR

Kishore Dharmarajan worked in the Advertising Industry for ten years before abandoning it for the digital space. Along the way, he wrote EIGHTSTORM, TWITTER CAN PAY YOUR MORTGAGE and now SNIPER MARKETING. Foolhardy enough to believe that he can create 100 books, he just has 97 more to go.

99% OF PEOPLE WHO READ THIS BOOK ARE GOING TO FORET THE PRINCIPLES IN THE NEXT FEW DAYS.

BUT THE 1% WHO ABSORB THE CONCEPTS ARE GOING TO STRIKE GOLD.

USE THE NOTES SECTION TO JOT DOWN

YOUR BEST IDEAS AND THEN APPLY SNIPER MARKETING TO IT.

YOU WILL SEE SUCCESS THAT YOU NEVER IMAGINED WAS POSSIBLE.

HAPPY SNIPING

_____

_____

_____

_____

_____

_____

_____

_____

_____

_____

KISHORE DHARMARAJAN

_____

_____

_____

_____

_____

_____

_____

_____

_____

_____

_____

_____

_____

_____

_____

_____

_____

_____

_____

_____

KISHORE DHARMARAJAN

_____

_____

_____

_____

_____

_____

_____

_____

_____

_____

KISHORE DHARMARAJAN

KISHORE DHARMARAJAN

KISHORE DHARMARAJAN

_____

_____

_____

_____

_____

_____

_____

_____

_____

_____

KISHORE DHARMARAJAN

_____

_____

_____

_____

_____

_____

_____

_____

_____

_____

_____

KISHORE DHARMARAJAN

_____

_____

_____

_____

_____

_____

_____

_____

_____

_____

_____

_____

_____

_____

_____

_____

_____

_____

_____

_____

_____

www.ingramcontent.com/pod-product-compliance
Lightning Source LLC
Chambersburg PA
CBHW072037190526
45165CB00017B/959

* 9 7 8 1 4 6 1 0 7 3 3 7 6 *